CELEBRATING THE FAMILY NAME OF YANG

Celebrating the Family Name of Yang

Walter the Educator

Silent King Books
a WhichHead Entertainment Imprint

Copyright © 2024 by Walter the Educator

All rights reserved. No part of this book may be reproduced in any manner whatsoever without written permission except in the case of brief quotations embodied in critical articles and reviews.

First Printing, 2024

Disclaimer

This book is a literary work; the story is not about specific persons, locations, situations, and/or circumstances unless mentioned in a historical context. Any resemblance to real persons, locations, situations, and/or circumstances is coincidental. This book is for entertainment and informational purposes only. The author and publisher offer this information without warranties expressed or implied. No matter the grounds, neither the author nor the publisher will be accountable for any losses, injuries, or other damages caused by the reader's use of this book. The use of this book acknowledges an understanding and acceptance of this disclaimer.

Celebrating the Family Name of Yang is a memory book that belongs to the Celebrating Family Name Book Series by Walter the Educator. Collect them all and more books at WaltertheEducator.com

USE THE EXTRA SPACE TO DOCUMENT YOUR FAMILY MEMORIES THROUGHOUT THE YEARS

YANG

In the balance of the earth and sky,

The name of Yang stands bold and high.

A harmony of strength and grace,

A family forged in time's embrace.

From sunrise hills to twilight streams,

The Yang name flows through ancient dreams.

A lineage deep, a spirit wide,

A legacy the years can't hide.

With roots in wisdom, bold and true,

The Yangs build futures fresh and new.

From fields they've tilled to stars they've charted,

A journey vast, where hope has started.

Beneath the moon's reflective glow,

The Yang name thrives, it will not slow.

Through shifting tides and winds that roar,

Their courage blooms forevermore.

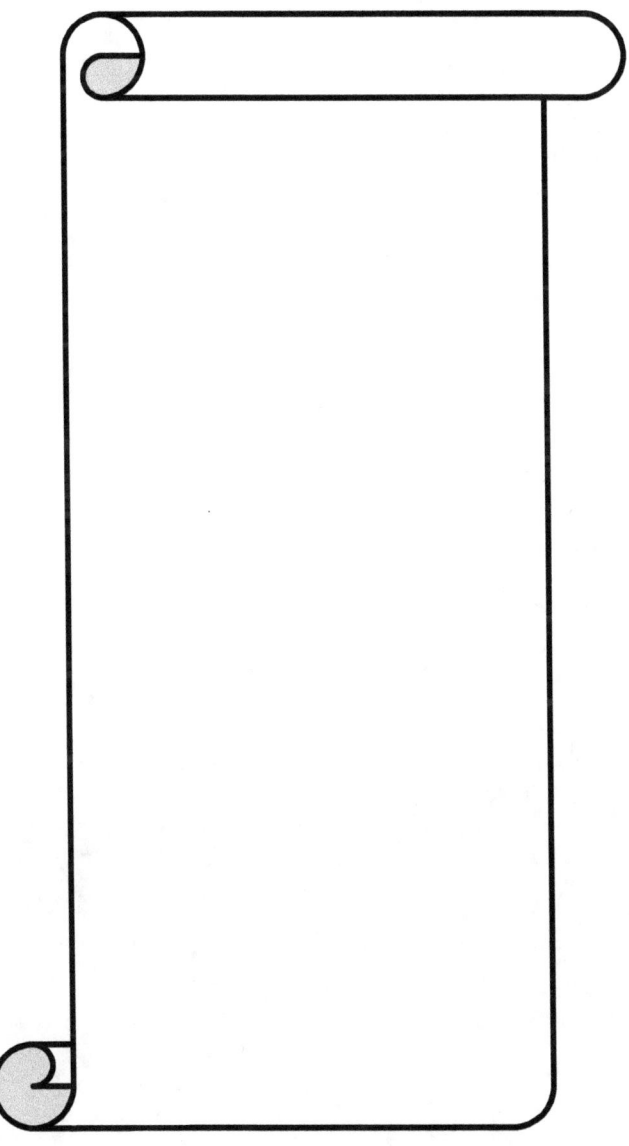

In village squares and bustling streets,

The Yangs' resolve no storm defeats.

A family bound by love's bright thread,

With every step, their path is spread.

From poets' quills to craftsmen's hands,

The Yang name shines across the lands.

Builders of dreams, defenders of light,

They forge a future, clear and bright.

Through trials faced, they stand as one,

With hearts as vast as the morning sun.

Each generation adds its part,

A beating drum, a steadfast heart.

Their name a melody, soft yet strong,

A rhythm echoing all day long.

The Yangs unite, through time they blend,

A story written without an end.

From golden fields to rivers wide,

The Yangs walk forward, side by side.

Their strength, their love, a beacon gleams,

A living testament to shared dreams.

So let us honor Yang's great name,

A family bound by time's bright flame.

Through every season, near and far,

The Yangs will shine, like a guiding star.

ABOUT THE CREATOR

Walter the Educator is one of the pseudonyms for Walter Anderson. Formally educated in Chemistry, Business, and Education, he is an educator, an author, a diverse entrepreneur, and he is the son of a disabled war veteran. "Walter the Educator" shares his time between educating and creating. He holds interests and owns several creative projects that entertain, enlighten, enhance, and educate, hoping to inspire and motivate you. Follow, find new works, and stay up to date with Walter the Educator™

at WaltertheEducator.com

www.ingramcontent.com/pod-product-compliance
Lightning Source LLC
LaVergne TN
LVHW052009060526
838201LV00059B/3931